STUCK in the Middle!

Puberty, Dating & Everything In Between

Published by SIP Publications, LLC.

Copyright © 2025 by J. Postell
ISBN: 979-8-9920972-3-8
Third Edition

All rights reserved. No part of this book may be reproduced in any form or by any means, electronic or mechanical, including photocopying, recording, or by any information storage and retrieval systems, without permission in writing from the authors, except where permitted by law and for reviews.

Cover Design: Matthew Postell

Printed in the United States of America

Contents

Introduction

Friendship & Puberty 1

Friendship Survey............................ 4

Puberty….. 7

Puberty Game 11

Dating 13

Peer Pressure 19

Emotional Steering & Bullying 28

Leaders…………………………….. 36

Leadership Quiz…………………… 41

Review………………………….... 44

Glossary………………………….. 46

Puberty Game Answer Key……..……. 48

Endnotes………………………… 50

STUCK in the Middle

It's not easy being a middle-schooler! The work is a lot harder than it was in elementary and there's a tremendous amount of homework. Puberty has come with a vengeance, and those hormones are alive and well! There's all these new weird emotions, awkward moments and random thoughts that flood your mind. Social media hasn't made it any easier. The days of private mistakes are over. Every mistake gets blasted over the internet for all the world to see, and finding your place in the world of friendships can seem like a reality show. How will you navigate this new territory in the journey of life?

The good news is, these changes you are going through are natural and temporary! With a roadmap and the right tools, you can successfully sail through your middle school years with great memories, lasting friendships and wisdom for the road ahead!

In the chapters ahead, you will be challenged to come out of your comfort zone, try new things and make new friends. You can also take the friendship survey, to see if you're being a good friend. Chapter 2 will define dating and discuss *love* vs. *infatuation*. Chapter 3 reveals the four types of peer pressure and how to deal with negative peer pressure. Chapter 4 discusses bullying, cyberbullying and bystanders, while Chapter 5 introduces you to emotional "steering" and manipulation. Turn to Chapter 6 and learn the methods to managing the negative emotions puberty can bring. Lastly, don't forget that you're a leader! So take the Leadership quiz in Chapter 7 and see how you score.

Fasten your seatbelts! Here we go!

Chapter 1

Friendship & Puberty

Do you have a hard time making friends?

Do you know how to make friends?

Have you made any new friends since entering middle school?

You may have a hard time making friends because you've never been taught. Making new friends is easier for social people but if you aren't as social, then striking up a conversation with someone new may be very intimidating. Listed below are a few ideas to get you started.

- **Compliment someone on something you like about them:** Complimenting people works almost every time. Once you genuinely compliment someone, they may compliment you back or strike up a conversation with you. Complimenting others shows your own confidence.

- **Ask someone new for help:** Believe it or not, asking for help from someone new, may lead to more conversation, which may lead to a friendship.

- **Introduce yourself:** Introducing yourself can be hard, but it shows others that you're approachable and friendly. This method also helps the other person let down their guard. Remember that other students are struggling with ways to approach friendship as well. Being the first person to open up to others could eventually lead to a blossoming friendship.

TRY NEW THINGS

Trying new things is a great way to meet new friends. It is also a great way to improve the quality of your life. Here are some things you can do to meet new people and possibly find people who share your interests:

- Join a club
- Volunteer
- Join study groups
- Join a sports team
- Get a hobby
- Start a club or group

Trying new things may feel awkward at first, but **push past it.** Being uncomfortable in a new environment or around new people is normal. Go with it. **Do not pull out your cell phone** to avoid the awkwardness of meeting new people. Reach out to people, be confident and see where it will lead you.

BEING A GOOD FRIEND

Remember that it is harder to make good friends than it is to lose them. If you aren't a good friend, you could soon find yourself friendless. Learning and modeling the behavior of a genuine friend will attract genuine friends.

The Friendship Code:

GOOD FRIENDS...

- Stand up for each other
- Encourage one another
- Stick together through hard times
- Communicate and work through conflict
- Listen without judgment
- Are honest, even when it is uncomfortable
- Respect each other's differences

GOOD FRIENDS DON'T...

- Gossip about each other
- Mistreat each other
- Betray one another's trust

Treat your friends as you would want them to treat you!

Friendship Survey
Are you a good friend?

1. Are you quick to help your friend(s)?
   Yes
   No

2. Do you sometimes talk negatively about your friend(s) to others?
   Yes
   No

3. Do you sometimes play cruel tricks on your friend(s)?
   Yes
   No

4. If you answered yes to question 3, how often do you play cruel tricks on your friend(s)?
   Rarely
   Somewhat often
   Often

5. Are you secretly jealous of your friend(s)?
   Yes
   No

6. Do you give your friend(s) good advice?
   Yes
   No

7. Do you and your friend(s) fight often?
   Yes
   No

8. Do you get easily angered at your friend(s)?
   Yes
   No

9. Do you tease your friend(s) with the intent to hurt them?
   Yes
   No

10. If you answered yes to question 9, how often do you tease your friend(s)?
    Rarely
    Somewhat often
    Often

11. When you've wronged your friend(s), are you quick to apologize?
    Yes
    No

12. Do you treat your friend(s) with respect?
    Yes
    No

*If you answered *yes* to questions **2, 3, 7, 8 and/or 9,** then you need to re-evaluate how you treat your friend(s). If you value friendship, then it should show. Good friendships will teach you about yourself, allow you to grow, and help shape you socially and emotionally.

Finding a good friend is difficult, especially in middle school. Friendship is crucial at any age, but particularly during adolescence. Teen movies never fail to cast the mean friend. Those movies are a true representation of what some teenage friendships are like.

Try your best to be a genuine friend. Don't be the **fake** or **mean** "friend" in the movie. Instead, try the dedicated friend role. It may sound corny, but there's nothing wrong with being a friend that others can count on.

Puberty[1]

Puberty: The process of physical changes (body changes) through which a child's body matures.

Your body and emotions are changing. It's called puberty, and you are **STUCK** smack dab in the middle of it!

Boys and girls will both experience puberty. Statistically, girls experience puberty between the ages of 8 and 13, and boys experience puberty between the ages of 9 and 15; however, some boys and girls experience puberty later.

Some of the physical changes in males and females due to puberty:

- Facial hair
- Voice changes
- Acne
- Body odor
- Brain development
- Attraction to others

Some of the emotional changes in males and females due to puberty:

- Mood swings
- Irritability
- Sensitivity
- Confusion
- Aggression
- Lack of self-confidence

Managing Your Emotions

Calmly stating your feelings without the negative emotions will allow for a better conversation. This is not always easy when you are feeling upset. Try the following ideas to help calm your emotions:

- **Count:** Counting to 10 or even 100 if needed, gives you time to calm down.

- **Take a walk:** Taking a walk can help reduce stress and calm you down.

- **Practice the conversation:** Rehearsing or writing down your thoughts before you have a conversation can help you better communicate your feelings.

- **Take deep breaths:** Taking deep breaths can help you calm down and relieve stress.

- **Get a hobby:** Take up sports, dance or writing. Hobbies help you let out all that pent up energy.

- **Calmly announce frustration and exit the situation:** Sometimes you need to leave a situation before it gets worse. Calmly state your emotion, quickly explain that you need to leave so that you can calm down and exit.

- **Arrange a time to revisit the conversation**: Once calm, talking through the situation can help the relationship grow stronger.

Why Do I Have These Emotions?

We develop emotional intelligence as we grow. Your brain is not fully developed until your early to mid-20's[2]. Emotional changes are due to the changes in your hormone levels. You won't feel stuck forever. Knowing how to avoid negative behaviors is key.

Try to AVOID negative behaviors like:

- Arguing
- Blaming
- Refusing to communicate
- Yelling
- Hitting
- Cursing
- Social Media: *Social media is not a good place to express your emotions. Calmly back away from the computer or put your phone down and wait until you are in a better mood to get on social media.*

Keeping Calm

Think about what keeps you calm. Write a few things down that help you to stay calm.

_____

_____

_____

_____

Remember that puberty is a natural process that helps us to develop into adults. Though it may seem physically and emotionally challenging during the process, you will find that your body was doing what was necessary to mature. Most kids during this age go through some ups and downs and uncertainty. This is natural, and you will feel more emotionally stable as you become older and hormones calm down.

STUCK in the Middle **Puberty Game**

Directions: Read each question carefully and circle the best answer. (To be played with the entire class)

1. During puberty, a guy's feet, arms, legs, and hands may grow faster than the rest of the body.
   True or False

2. The average age for puberty to begin in boys is between...
   a. 10-14
   b. 9-15
   c. 5-14

3. Aggression is one of the emotional changes that happens in guys and girls during puberty.
   True or False

4. Hormones are:
   a. Chemicals in the body that control the changes that occur during puberty.
   b. The process of physical changes through which a child's body matures.
   c. Changes that happen in life.

5. Estrogen is the predominant hormone in females.
   True or False

6. Who should you talk to about the changes you experience during puberty?
   a. parents
   b. older siblings

      c. teacher
      d. grandmother
      e. All of the above

7. **The gland in the brain that triggers puberty is…**
      a. testosterone
      b. pituitary gland
      c. thyroid gland

8. **You will need MORE sleep during puberty?**
True or False

9. **It is uncommon to experience major mood swings during puberty.**
True or False

10. **Testosterone is the predominant hormone in males.**
True or False

11. **During puberty, it is common for a male's vocal tone to get high for an instant while speaking. What is this called?**
      a. cracking
      b. soprano
      c. high pitch

12. **What is the best way to manage your negative emotions?**
      a. take a walk & take deep breaths
      b. log on to Instagram & exercise
      c. run somewhere & take karate lessons

Chapter 2
Dating

What is dating?

_____
_____
_____
_____

How do you know when you're ready to start dating someone?

_____
_____
_____
_____

What are some qualities or characteristics you look for in someone you want to date?

_____
_____
_____
_____

What do you say to the person you are interested in dating? (The BIG Ask)

_____

_____

_____

_____

What age should you start to date?

_____

_____

_____

_____

What is the purpose of dating?

_____

_____

_____

_____

*What is **your** definition of love?*

_____

_____

_____

_____

Love: *Willing the good of the other for their own sake, and not for one's own benefit; An intense feeling of deep affection.*

How do you know when you're in love with someone?

_____

_____

Infatuation: An intense but **short-lived** passion or admiration for someone or something.

An infatuation involves being interested in, fascinated by, or obsessed with another person. Most people believe they're in love, but they're really infatuated with the person. They have intense feelings for the person just like love, but it is temporary.

Infatuation is usually based on being attracted to someone. They may love how the person looks, behaves or what they can provide. Infatuation may make you believe someone is perfect when they are not.

What can you do to make sure you're in love and not infatuated with someone?

_____

_____

_____

_____

Take time to get to know the person. Don't make long-term decisions based on an intense - possibly temporary - moment. Only time will tell you if you really love someone or if you just have a major crush on them (infatuation).

Spending time with others will reveal who they really are. You may think someone is nice but after spending time with that person, you may learn they're not as they appeared to be. Taking the time to get to know someone can help you to avoid painful breakups and heartaches.

Abusive Relationship Red Flags

If you are experiencing any of these in your dating relationship, tell someone and seek help immediately.

- Invasion of your privacy
- Says hurtful things to you
- Forces you to kiss, hug or have sex with them
- Acts envious, possessive or controlling
- Makes you feel afraid
- Physically hurts you in any way
- Calls or texts you constantly
- Becomes angry if you say "No"
- Does not want you to hang out with friends or family members
- Threatens to hurt themselves or someone else if you don't do what they say
- Constantly blames you for problems in the relationship, and not taking any responsibility for the same

Teen Dating Violence Hotline: 1-866-331-9474

Remedy Live 24/7 chat line: Text 494949 to chat with a real person

Activity:

1. Make two separate lists.

    - List 3 or 4 characteristics that you desire in a friend. *(i.e. "fun", "creative", etc.)*
    - Now, make a list of characteristics you desire in the person you date.

2. Compare.

    - Compare the characteristics you made for a friend, with the list of characteristics you made for the person you choose to date.

Do some of the characteristics match? **They should!**

The person you choose to date should have some of the same characteristics you desire in a friend. If you wouldn't choose the person you're dating as a friend, then you shouldn't date them. Compromising your **must-haves** in your relationships could eventually lead to disappointment.

Don't jump into a friendship or relationship with just anyone. Evaluate their qualities. See if they have any of your **must haves**. Do NOT compromise your values! If the person doesn't meet your requirements, move on. Eventually you will meet someone with whom you are more compatible.

Chapter 3

Peer Pressure

Peer Pressure: Influence from members of one's peer group.

Have you ever experienced peer pressure?

Most teenagers will experience some form of peer pressure in their life. Feeling the need to fit in, lack of maturity and wanting to be liked are just a few reasons teens give in to some of these pressures. Understanding the types of peer pressure can help you avoid making a decision you may later regret.

Types of Peer Pressure:

- **Spoken:** A peer verbally influences you to do something you may not want to do. (i.e. "Everybody is doing it" or "What's the big deal?')

- **Unspoken:** You observe your peers doing something you know is not right. (i.e. Drinking, doing drugs or witnessing inappropriate social media or text messages.)

- **Negative:** You are negatively influenced to do something you are uncomfortable with in order to fit in. (i.e. Gossiping about a friend.)

- **Positive:** Peer pressure is not always negative. You can be positively influenced by your peers. (i.e. Seeing others stand up for someone, playing sports or receiving encouragement to meet your goals.)

List the activities that teens are pressured into:

_____

_____

_____

_____

_____

Peer Pressure & Sexual Activity

List ways to avoid being peer pressured into doing things, such as kissing, or sexual touching

_____

_____

_____

_____

_____

Do you feel pressured to try things that are sexual?

If someone genuinely cares for you, they will respect your decision to **wait**. Sex does not equal love. Do not compromise your values for the acceptance of others. Take your time and get to know the person before making a decision that will affect you and your future. **You are worth waiting for!**

Peer Pressure & Drugs

How can you be peer pressured into trying drugs?

- In a 2024 survey 10% of 8th grade students reported vaping nicotine, with 4.5% saying they vaped nicotine regularly[3]

- On average, kids try drugs for the first time when they're between the ages of 13 and 15.[3]

- The younger someone is when they try drugs, the more likely they are to become addicted.[4]

Define each drug listed below:

What is an "over-the-counter" drug?

_____

_____

What is a "prescription" drug?

_____

_____

What are "illegal" drugs?

_____

_____

What could be the danger of accepting medication offered by a friend?

_____

_____

Why do you think some of your peers use drugs and alcohol?

_____

_____

What are some consequences of using drugs and alcohol?

Why is it a good idea for teens to wait until they are 21 before they drink alcohol?

- Research shows that those who began drinking before age 14 years 47% developed an addiction, but people that waited until after 21 only 9% experienced lifetime dependence[5]

- Alcohol is the most common substance abused by middle schoolers. In 2024, 18.5 percent of eighth-graders surveyed said they had drunk alcohol at some point, and 6.7 percent report having been drunk in their lifetime.[3]

*Name **two** things you would like to accomplish by the time you graduate high school.*

1.

2.

What are some ways drugs and alcohol can interfere with your goals after high school?

_____

_____

_____

_____

Peer pressure is often **unavoidable**; however when you have tools that help you to know how to respond, it eases the pressure to give in and builds your confidence.

Ways to handle negative peer pressure:

- **Be assertive:** Saying "no" communicates your boundaries. People are less likely to try to pressure you into doing things when you verbalize your boundaries and stick to them.

- **Have an escape plan:** When approached with negative peer pressure, you need to have a plan in place that can help you escape the negative situation.

- **Choose good friends:** Your circle of friends is important. Hanging with good people can help you avoid the dangers of peer pressure.

- **Flip it:** When you are approached with negative peer pressure, flip it. Offer positive suggestions instead. Don't worry about being made fun of because of your choices. Be a leader and encourage others to do the same. Later on in life, nobody laughs at the person who is doing well!

Peer Pressure & Individuality

Did you know that it is healthy to be unique?

You have your own set of unique qualities that make you who you are. People may try to make you feel bad or act as if you're awkward because you don't do everything they do. Awkward moments are a normal part of being a teenager. Your school years will be full of awkward moments, but it's important to push past them and be yourself. Being unique makes you interesting and fun! Embrace the things that make you different. See those things as a way to contribute to the world around you in a special way!

List a few things about yourself that make you unique.

_____

_____

_____

Name some characteristics that you appreciate about people who are different from you.

_____

_____

_____

Pressured to be Mature

Have you ever been told to act your age?

One-minute people expect you to be mature, and the next minute, they remind you that you are still a child. This can be very confusing.

You're in between elementary and high school. At this stage in your development, your body, emotions, school life, and possibly your personal life, have changed radically. You're stuck! This is why we call the program, "Stuck in the Middle." Being stuck at this stage of development can be difficult, but it's all part of the growing process.

At this stage you may feel too old for some of the things you did back in elementary; but let's be honest, some of it is still fun! There is nothing wrong with enjoying some of the things you did when you were younger!

Who doesn't love a game of "musical chairs"? Going around and around to the beat, while waiting for the music to stop so that you can be the first to snag a seat, is fun at any age!

Don't be afraid to be yourself. You may feel stuck at this stage of development but that doesn't mean you have to be stuck in the expectations of others. It's okay to be who you are and where you are right now.

List some activities that you still enjoy doing. (Feel free to share your list with others - it doesn't matter whether it seems "mature" or not.)

Example: Skating

1. _____

2. _____

3. _____

4. _____

5. _____

6. _____

7. _____

8. _____

9. _____

10. _____

Chapter 4
Emotional Steering & Bullying

Emotional Steering: Masterfully steering someone's mind and emotions a certain way to gain power over them.

-Can you be emotionally manipulated in your friendships or dating relationship? **YES!**

If someone has tried to manipulate you into doing things you don't want to do, you might be a victim of *emotional steering*. Emotional steering is equivalent to the puppet and the puppet master. The "steerer" knows exactly what to say and do to gain power over you. Like the puppet master, they know that pulling certain strings will change your emotions. Understanding the strategies used by a steerer will help you to avoid falling prey to their manipulation.

Who Can Be an Emotional Steerer?
- Any age
- Any ethnicity
- Any gender

...Anyone can be an emotional steerer!

Following is a list of emotional steering strategies used by a steerer to get what they want from you. Learn each strategy to avoid becoming a victim.

Emotional Steering Strategies:

Emotional steerers are relentless. They will first try using **C.C.E.U.** *If that doesn't work, they will move on to a more aggressive approach.*

- **C- Charm:** The steerer will say and do whatever necessary to gain power over you. **(i.e. Constantly says things that make you feel like you are the most important person in the world, and then asks for something in return.)**

- **C- Coax**: The steerer will try to gently, yet persistently, persuade you to get what they want. **(i.e. Offer money or things, get you to do their homework for them, etc.)**

- **E- Entice:** The steerer will try to entice you by offering you gifts in order to get what they want. **(i.e. Physical advances or relationships beyond friendships.)**

- **U- Us against the world:** When using the "us-against-the-world" strategy, the steerer will say things like, "We only have each other," or "Nobody loves you like I do." The goal with this strategy is to gain your utmost trust, to get what they want. **(i.e. Spending time with you alone, pulls you away from family time, isolates you from your friends, and pressures you to trust them early in the relationship.)**

With every rejection given, the steerer becomes increasingly desperate. Their strategies intensify from subtle manipulation to full-out aggression. From **C.C.E.U.**, the steerer moves to **I.P.T.L**

- **I- Ignoring:** The steerer uses this strategy to rile up their victim, in an attempt to make the victim feel they have done something wrong. This is a passive-aggressive way of getting what the "steerer" has been demanding from the victim.

- **P- Provoking:** The steerer's goal is to get the victim to act outside of their character. They want to provoke the victim to act a certain way, so they can later guilt them into getting what they want.

- **T- Threats:** This strategy is used by the most aggressive type of steerer, the bully. He or she may begin bullying the victim by using empty threats to get them to do what they want.

- **L- Lying (Slander):** Aggressive steerers have been known to lie or slander their victim's names and/or character, to get what they want.

Know & No: How to STOP the Emotional Steerer

- **Know:** Once you **know** the strategies you can avoid being a victim. Also, **know** when to seek out help! If you are trapped in a toxic relationship, talk to a trusted adult.

- **No:** Saying, "No!" to the steerer stops him or her in their tracks. Say it confidently, as a steerer may sense your uncertainty and will continue if you aren't firm.

Bullying

Bullying: Verbal, physical, and/or mental acts committed by a person to harass, intimidate or cause harm to another person.

Fact: 2 in 10 U.S. students say they have been bullied in school. [6]

Fact: Most bullying happens in middle school. The most common types were being made the subject of rumors and being made fun of, called names or insulted. [7]

Cyberbullying: The use of electronic communication to bully a person, typically by sending messages of an intimidating or threatening nature.

Fact: Nearly 46% of kids have been bullied online. 1 in 4 has had it happen more than once. [8]

Fact: On average 25% of children have admitted to cyberbullying others. [9]

Why do you think people bully others?

Why Bullies Bully:

- To fit in
- Jealousy
- Peer pressure
- They are victims of bullying
- Fear
- Want control or power
- Mental instability

Bullying is Abuse!

Victims of bullying show some of the same negative effects as victims of abuse. Victims should be supported, and abusers should be reported immediately.

Can you tell someone is a bully just by looking at them?

No, you can't tell a bully - or a victim of bullying - by simply looking at them. Bullies and their victims come in all sizes, ages, ethnicities and genders. Don't be fooled by a certain look. You can only spot a bully when they're committing the act.

Bullying and Suicide

Fact: The suicide rate among kids ages 10 to 14 has been steadily rising.[11]

Bullying is a traumatizing experience for victims, which can result in emotional and physical scars. Bullying can lead to feelings of helplessness, despair and utter hopelessness. **If you or someone you know are experiencing any of these feelings, tell someone immediately! Tell until someone listens. The way to put a stop to the bullying and possibly save someone's life, is to report it to a trusted adult and ask for help!**

Remember:
- You are not alone.
- You are valuable.
- You are needed.

Speak Up! Step Up! Stand Up!

-Speak Up!: Don't stand for abusive behavior. Report it to a trusted adult as soon as it starts. Reporting it to a parent/guardian, teacher, coach or other trusted adult empowers you to get the help and support you need and deserve!

-Step Up: Tell bullies "NO!" Let them know that you will not be an easy target. Let them know that their bullying is wrong and that you will stand up for yourself. Once a bully knows you are confident, they no longer have the upper hand. Be bold! Show the love you have for yourself. If a bully thinks you have low self-esteem, they will try their best to intimidate you.

-Stand Up: Not only should you stand up against being bullied, but you should also stand up for others who are being bullied. Don't ignore bullying. By reporting bullying, you show the victim that you care, and send a message that you will not be a bystander.

Bystander: A person who is present at an event or incident but does not take part.

57% of the time, bullying stops within 10 seconds when a bystander intervenes[12].

Kids who witness bullying are more likely to:[10]
- Have increased use of tobacco, alcohol, or other drugs
- Have increased mental health problems including

depression and anxiety.
- Miss or skip school.

If **YOU** are the Bully:

Change the negative behavior! Bullies tend to be insecure on the inside, so they act out to help themselves feel better. Maybe you were abused, so you are acting out how you have been treated. You may feel angry or out of control, and do not know why you treat others the way you do. You may not know how to calm your emotions. The most important thing you can do is to talk to someone and seek help for yourself before you or your victim does something that cannot be reversed. Only **YOU** can decide to take a step toward change and stop bullying!

What will you do to help end bullying?

_____

_____

_____

Fact: 44.2% of students that report being bullied during school notify a trusted adult. 6th grade students were most likely to talk to an adult, but by 12th grade only 32% asked for help[7]

Why Aren't Victims Talking?

- **Fear:** Some teens fear what may happen if they tell. Don't be afraid to report bullies. It's one of the only ways to STOP them. You are doing the right thing! Don't fear retaliation. Most bullies get away with bullying because they don't believe their victims will tell anyone.

- **Unawareness:** Cyberbullying is bullying. Just because it is happening online, through text or through email does not make it any different. Bullying is bullying.

- **Shame:** You may feel ashamed of the mistreatment, but being bullied is NOT your fault. No one deserves to be bullied. Make sure to report cyberbullying immediately.

- **No Escape:** There is a way out! Tell a trusted adult about cyberbullying. Once reported, there are actions that can be taken to stop the bullying.

Don't ignore bullying. Stand up against those that commit these acts. Report bullying the minute you witness it.

Tips for reporting bullying:
- Ask a trusted adult if they will listen to your story.
- Give as many details as you can remember.
- Ask what will happen next.
- If you do not have anyone you can trust, or want to remain anonymous, call a helpline:

Stop Bullying Now Helpline 1-800-273-8255

Suicide National Lifeline 1-800-784-2433

Emergency or Immediate Danger? Call 911!

https://www.stopbullying.gov/kids

Chapter 5

Leaders

What excites you most about going to high school?

What are you most nervous about?

What will you miss most about middle school?

What is your definition of a leader?

_____

_____

_____

_____

What does it take to be a good leader?

_____

_____

_____

Who can be a leader?

_____

_____

_____

_____

There are **two types** of leaders:

1. **Intentional Leader:** An intentional leader makes purposeful decisions. They are deliberate in what they do and what they stand for.

2. **Accidental Leader:** An accidental leader is thrust into leadership by chance or by opportunity. They may have

been forced into leadership by standing up or speaking up on someone's behalf.

Which type of leader best describes your leadership style? Give an example of a time you chose to or had to be a leader.

What is your definition of a follower?

Is a follower viewed in a positive or negative light? Why?

When is being a follower a bad thing? Can it sometimes be a good thing to be a follower?

_____

_____

_____

Why do some people choose to follow instead of lead?

_____

_____

_____

Good leaders set goals. Write 4 goals of a good leader.

1.

2.

3.

4.

Do you think that setting future school/career goals are important? Why or why not?

_____

_____

_____

_____

What are some future school or career goals that you can set?

_____

_____

_____

_____

_____

Leadership Quiz

1. I like it when people share their opinions.
Often-3 Sometimes-2 Rarely-1

2. I do what's best for the group.
Often-3 Sometimes-2 Rarely-1

3. I respect other people's opinions, even if they're different from mine.
Often-3 Sometimes-2 Rarely-1

4. I tell people that they have great ideas.
Often-3 Sometimes-2 Rarely-1

5. I try to consider everyone's feelings in the group.
Often-3 Sometimes-2 Rarely-1

6. I stay calm when people disagree with me.
Often-3 Sometimes-2 Rarely-1

7. When there's a problem I don't blame others.
Often-3 Sometimes-2 Rarely-1

8. I take the advice of others.
Often-3 Sometimes-2 Rarely-1

Scoring:

20-24 points: You're a great leader! Keep helping others.

12-19 points: You have a lot of good leadership skills! Keep at it. You are on your way to becoming a great leader!

8-11 points: Keep practicing. Look back at this quiz to get an idea of what areas you need to work on. Remember, great leaders are always open to learning and growing!

Good Leaders:

- Communicate.
- Listen.
- Learn.
- Work hard.
- Give & take advice.
- Inspire others.
- Set a good example.
- Have control over their emotions.

Leadership isn't about what a person looks like, nor is it about what a person has. Good character makes you a good leader. Soon you will be entering high school, and you will need to be a leader BEFORE you get there. Don't wait until you are a senior in high school to show your leadership ability.
Start off strong, so you end even stronger. ***Leaders don't wait to be told to lead, they do it naturally.***

Remember:

- You are NEEDED!
- You are IMPORTANT!
- You will do GREAT THINGS!
- You will meet GREAT PEOPLE!
- You will go to GREAT PLACES!
- You are NOT **STUCK**!

You are smack-dab in the **MIDDLE** of learning about who you are and that is exactly where you are supposed to be!!!

Review:

Remember some of the friendships you build now will likely carry over into high school. Be good to your friends. Don't forget the friendship code from Chapter 1.

You're a pre-teen or a teenager, so enjoy it! Get out of those teenage blues. You'll only be a teenager for seven years of your entire life. The years go by quickly. Don't waste them. Play a game of Musical Chairs, go skating, dance yourself silly. Have fun! You're only as stuck as you feel.

Puberty is a part of the developmental process. Everyone goes through it. You can manage the negative emotions you feel by using the strategies we've discussed in Chapter 1. Practicing these strategies will help you better manage your emotions.

Your physical changes will run their course. Be patient and know that once you get through puberty, you will feel much better and more confident about yourself!

Be wise when choosing someone to date. If you wouldn't choose them to be your friend, then don't date them! Do not compromise your wants for anyone. You are valuable and you need to be treated as such.

Most teens will face some form of peer pressure in high school. Using the tools you learned in Chapter 3 will help you to resist negative pressures. Remember to have a plan in place when approached with negative peer pressure.

Watch out for emotional steering. Revisit the strategies that Steerers use on their victims. Say "No!" to steerers and their manipulative ways. Share the strategies with your friends that may be in emotionally abusive relationships. Most people don't know they're a victim of emotional steering until they're made aware.

Stand up to bullying! Be bold! Be confident! You don't have to be a victim. Fight for yourself and for others. Your middle school years should be filled with great memories, not lasting regrets. (Visit **www.stopbullying.gov**)

Everyone is a leader! Great leaders find great people to follow. Being a leader in your generation is what makes the world a better place. Take the time to think about how you can help someone, start a group that fights for something you believe in, or take a stand against something that is harming your peers.

GLOSSARY

Friendship: The emotions or conduct of friends; a relationship between friends.

Puberty: The process of physical changes (body changes) through which a child's body matures.

Dating: Seeing somebody specific with purpose and on a regular basis.

Love: Willing the good of the other for their own sake, and not for one's own benefit; An intense feeling of deep affection

Infatuation: An intense but short-lived passion or admiration for someone or something.

Peer Pressure: Influence from members of one's peer group.

Emotional Steering: Masterfully steering someone's emotions a certain way to gain power over them. (A form of mental and emotional abuse)

Bullying: Verbal, physical or mental acts committed by a person to harass, intimidate or cause harm to another person.

Bystander: A person who is present at an event or incident but does not take part

Cyberbullying: The use of electronic communication to bully a person, typically by sending messages of an intimidating or threatening nature.

Leader: Someone whom other people will follow.

Intentional leader: An intentional leader makes purposeful decisions. They are deliberate in what they do and what they stand for.

Accidental leader: An accidental leader is thrust into leadership by chance or by opportunity. They may have been forced into leadership by standing up or speaking up on someone's behalf.

Follower: A person who moves or travels behind someone or something.

Puberty Game Answer Key

1. **During puberty, a guy's feet, arms, legs, and hands may grow faster than the rest of the body.**

   TRUE

2. **The average age for puberty to begin in boys is between...**

   b. 9-15

3. **Aggression is one of the emotional changes that happens in guys and girls during puberty.**

   TRUE

4. **Hormones are:**

   a. Chemicals in the body that control the changes that occur during puberty.

5. **Estrogen is the predominant hormone in females.**

   TRUE

6. **Who should you talk to about the changes you experience during puberty?**

   e. All of the above

7. **The gland in the brain that triggers puberty is...**

   b. pituitary gland

8. True or False: You will need MORE sleep during puberty?

   TRUE

9. It is uncommon to experience major mood swings during puberty.

   FALSE

10. Testosterone is the predominant hormone in males.

    TRUE

11. During puberty, it is common for a male's vocal tone to get high for an instant while speaking. What is this called?

    a. cracking

12. What is the best way to manage your negative emotions?

    a. take a walk & take deep breaths

ENDNOTES

1. Breehl L, Caban O. Physiology, Puberty. [Updated 2023 Mar 27]. In: StatPearls [Internet]. Treasure Island (FL): StatPearls Publishing; 2025 Jan-. Available from: https://www.ncbi.nlm.nih.gov/books/NBK534827/

2. National Institute of Mental Health. (2023). *The Teen Brain: 7 Things to Know - National Institute of Mental Health (NIH Publication No. 23-MH-8078)*. U.S. Department of Health and Human Services, National Institutes of Health. https://www.nimh.nih.gov/health/publications/the-teen-brain-7-things-to-know

3. Miech, R. A., Johnston, L. D., Patrick, M. E., & O'Malley, P. M. (2025). Monitoring the Future national survey results on drug use, 1975–2024: Overview and detailed results for secondary school students. Monitoring the Future Monograph Series. Ann Arbor, MI: Institute for Social Research, University of Michigan. https://monitoringthefuture.org/wpcontent/uploads/2024/12/mtf2025.pdf

4. Chloe J. Jordan, Susan L. Andersen, Sensitive periods of substance abuse: Early risk for the transition to dependence, Developmental Cognitive Neuroscience, Volume 25, 2017, Pages 29-44, ISSN 1878-9293, https://doi.org/10.1016/j.dcn.2016.10.004.

5. Hingson RW, Heeren T, Winter MR. Age at Drinking Onset and Alcohol Dependence: Age at Onset, Duration, and Severity. Arch Pediatr Adolesc Med. 2006;160(7):739–746. https://doi.org/10.1001/archpedi.160.7.739

6. Schaeffer, K. (2023, November 17). *9 facts about bullying in the U.S.* Pew Research Center. https://www.pewresearch.org/short-reads/2023/11/17/9-facts-about-bullying-in-the-us/

ENDNOTES

7. National Center for Education Statistics. (2024). Student Bullying. Condition of Education. U.S. Department of Education, Institute of Education Sciences. https://nces.ed.gov/programs/coe/indicator/a10.

8. Vogels, E. A. (2022, December 15). *Teens and Cyberbullying 2022*. Pew Research Center. https://www.pewresearch.org/internet/2022/12/15/teens-and-cyberbullying-2022/

9. Zhu, C., Huang, S., Evans, R., & Zhang, W. (2021). Cyberbullying Among Adolescents and Children: A Comprehensive Review of the Global Situation, Risk Factors, and Preventive Measures. *Frontiers in public health*, 9, 634909. https://doi.org/10.3389/fpubh.2021.634909

10. *Effects of Bullying*. (2025, February 03). StopBullying.gov. https://www.stopbullying.gov/bullying/effects

11. Curtin, S. C., & Garnett, M. F. (2023, June 15). *Products - Data Briefs - Number 471 - June10 2023*. CDC. https://www.cdc.gov/nchs/products/databriefs/db471.htm

12. Polanin, J.R., Espelage, D.L., & Pigott, T.D. (2012). A meta-analysis of school-based bullying prevention programs' effects on bystander intervention behavior. School Psychology Review, 41, 47-65. https://www.tandfonline.com/doi/full/10.1080/02796015.2012.12087375

www.ingramcontent.com/pod-product-compliance
Lightning Source LLC
Chambersburg PA
CBHW061421300426
44114CB00015B/2015